AF480786

Voices of Many

Voices of Many

POEMS FOR EVERY SOUL

Dean

ISBN: 979-8-89228-351-9   (Paperback)
ISBN: 979-8-89228-352-6   (Paperback)
ISBN: 979-8-89228-353-3   (eBook)

Book Ordering Information:
Atticus Publishing
548 Market St PMB 70756
San Francisco, CA 94104
(888) 208-9296
info@atticuspublishing.com
www.atticuspublishing.com

Contents

August 31, 2023

Brandon and Nikki

Brandon and Nikki, I'm glad to see you accomplished this day, August 31, 2023.

You seem to make the perfect pair. No matter what people think Hell you don't care.

Thank you for letting us be a part of your day. We love, honor, and support you in every way.

There is more to life than freedom of speech. Your young Ass's have a life to teach.

I know you're happy, I see it in your eyes. You love each other and that's no surprise.

You help each other through thick and thin when you can't you have the girls, Boyd and Finn.

Remember to always make your anniversaries count. That will keep you together through the trials you mount.

Your love will grow stronger every day. A job to work on but it's ok.

Mr. and Mrs. Gresham

Cheers to Mr. and Mrs. Gresham in 2023. Oct 28th Cole and Savanah that would be.

You took a while to get to this day. No more complaining from me {anyways}.

To the bride for a happier ever-after life. To the groom for making her his beautiful wife.

I wish you the best cause that's what moms do. If you need anything you know who to turn to,

I don't want the tears to come out and burst. So Cole I'll let you know I loved her first.

I've been waiting for you to become my son. I promised you something, so I'm not done.

A picture of the gift for I couldn't bring it here. It's so big and huge, that doesn't sound right, I fear.

You know who would want you to have it' So you find the spot to make it fit.

Thank you, Cole, for blessing me twice Making Savanah your bride and my sweet angel.

You'll be an awesome husband and an amazing Dad. A son you've been that I haven't had.

Savanah baby girl it's hard letting you go. Tears I'm holding back though you already know.

I believe you and Cole are the perfect match. Being best friends and he's an amazing catch.

Savanah, I'm happy for you. All your dreams have now come true.

A beautiful bride and an amazing Mom. Juni is beautiful and her personality's the bomb.

Mr. and Mrs. Gresham

No matter what you'll always be our little------. Let me just say it rhymes with bloopers.

Sorry to embarrass you just a bit. But you know I had to do it.

Seriously congratulations to the bride and groom. Best dressed couple in the entire room.

Best wishes to both and your eternal life. Cheers and congrats to the Husband and wife.

Be Strong, Not Weak

Money's complicated, why can't I let it go? It's wanted and needed, and I hate it so.

Forgive me for not being so free. Money doesn't fall from trees.

I do my best to help when I can. With kids our troops, my heart's in their hands.

My guilt is killing me, please make it stop. I'm sowing my seeds and haven't harvested a crop.

When I can give without worry or fret, I'll be living a life without debt.

I know you can help it happened before. If I let go and let God, it will help for sure.

Please touch my heart with your will. Please make this stress no big deal

Please Lord help me to be strong and not weak. When asked, ''help me not freak.

Prayers by Claudine.

Growing Strong

I'm alone for the first time.

Sometimes it feels like a crime.

I'm not looking but getting a lot of bites

The list of maybes or mights.

Need to find myself and be happy.

It's sad to sit alone and be free.

Writing brings out the best in me.

Having the free time is good! Si.

Most of my friends have live-ins.

So, they have a company under their Tins.

I will live cause that's what I choose.

Men and sex are something I can lose.

I am growing strong.

I will find where I belong.

Family Bond

I'm young yet strong, Monsters and Super Market Flowers are my favorite songs.

The artists are James Blunt and Ed Sheeran, take a listen you'll thank me for sharing.

My culture may intimidate you. Get to know me, you'll like me too.

Lost my grandma at the age of fourteen. I have a family bond that some have never seen.

The name Sanchez says it all. Proud of my background, makes me stand tall.

I shared my feelings with a special friend. Thank you, Claudine, for the message you sent.

Thanks for getting to know me. There's more if you want there to be.

I have a hookup and you can too. Contact Claudine and see what she can do.

Take care and God bless. May your life be stressless.

Complicated

Why is life so complicated, many things I totally hated.

Trying to put the pieces together, is not easy under the weather.

I poured out my heart and got the shaft.

You took everything I got the raft.

You think I'm stupid by the things you say.

You keep taking, so I walked away.

Thank you for being who you are.

You can't stop me, I'll go far.

No more hellos or goodbyes.

Enough of your stupid lies.

I'm glad it's over and we are through.

Leave me alone, I'm done with you.

I like you a lot.

Intense

You're so intense if you only knew.

What goes through my mind and what you do.

The slightest touch sends chills it seems.

Catch myself in a series of daydreams.

No matter what we will remain friends.

That is the bond we carry 'til the end.

Heart goes pitter-patter, heads full of bliss.

Vow we made so I promise you this.

Hanging out is our fav, I'd say that's fair.

Chances are something we don't dare.

Keeping things locked up is tough.

Finding time is a little rough.

Wish we could talk more as friends.

Are you afraid of the message it sends?

So you know I got your back.

Friendship is more important [fact!]

Blindside

Feeling like we are through.

Then I don't know what to do.

You do this thing and reel me in.

Confuses me now and then.

Play me once I give you a chance.

Play me twice it's not the same dance.

A simple text is all it takes.

Can you do that for heaven's sake?

Friendship is all I ask for.

You have this wall without a door.

What's the secret, why do you try to hide.

I'm a passing car on your blind side.

I'm here when you need a friend.

Why is it not the same message you send?

I got the hint, time to walk away.

Will you regret it or miss it someday?

Try Not To Panic

Meeting that someone is unique.

Makes you quiver or somewhat freak.

Try not to panic for it's just a dream.

What would your spouse say, yell or scream.

Don't see the face or know the name.

Hearing the voice and the smell wild but tame.

Erotic visions dancing in my head.

Waiting for the next episode while lying in bed.

Exciting as it sounds it's just a dream.

Passionate fantasies throughout it seems.

No foul play or pursuit at fault.

Desires we long for like tequila with salt.

Now you see things in a different way.

Broaden your horizon and drift away.

The passion has opened another door.

Relax and enjoy cause there's so much more.

Chemistry

Two people stuck in a web.

Perfect as long as they are in bed.

One's a romantic the other is not.

The chemistry is so damn hot.

Make the perfect puzzle, just missing a piece.

No romantic connection, stuck in a web capeesh?

Hopefully, they can get through this.

This is something they both could miss.

Romantic thinks it through and understands.

They're better off as friends.

Thanks for helping with self-esteem.

Opening up and saying more things.

Communication is another key.

Understanding where you're coming from, see?

Somehow, someway we will make it through.

This is what they've chosen to do.

Every Rainbow

A piece of my heart is gone forever.

The bond we had was like no other.

The bruising and agony how could you main Tain.

I'm so amazed at how you endured the pain.

Your smile lit up when I walked into the room.

My heart was breaking knowing you'd leave me soon.

Cracking jokes and talking about the past.

Watching Gilmore Girls and praying it would last.

R2gen2 was a penguin from the zoo she met.

Along with the sounds from King Lewie.

All are part of the bucket list Dannielle set.

Glam and game night is played along with a movie.

Every rainbow I'll think of you.

The peace and color it holds, are purple pink, and blue.

It's hard to be an auntie without her niece.

You fought hard, now rest in peace

LOVE AUNTIE DEAN

Faults

Things aren't like they used to be.

Surrounded by people that loved me.

No more trying to please you.

And no more telling me what to do.

Once you realize my heart is gone.

Take your lives and just move on.

It's a shame I must feel this way.

Not having my back and the things you say.

Not everyone's shoes fit the same.

Playing with my heart is not a game.

You as well are grown adults.

The mirror shows all our faults.

Sorry, I'm so blunt and speak my mind.

I see that in all of you, I tend to find.

Forgive me for making your lives a total hell.

Sorry for putting you under my spell.

Sorrow

Mother of six trying to survive.

Only four are alive.

One murdered and miscarried another.

She lives her life for the others.

Twinkie, I wish you the best in your future.

The pain and suffering sting worse than the suture.

Robbed at gunpoint, but still going strong.

Old school to that's how we live so long.

Holding back the sorrows from your green-eyed angel.

Makes your heart hurt and your hands dangle.

Losing someone you love so much.

You go numb and out of touch.

Bless you for what you're going through.

I know how you feel, I'm going through it too.

It never gets easier; you just learn to deal.

I hope you find it in your heart to heal.

Love and wishes

Claudine Donaldson

Testomony

Happiness starts when you want it to.

The choice is yours to make.

Make a change or just be you.

You don't have to be phony or fake.

Depression sucks some won't understand.

Take a deep breath and count to ten.

You opened the door to a new friend.

Now it's time for life to begin.

Anthony your testimony is like walking the plank.

Fingers blown off and shot point blank.

Thank you for sharing your threatening ordeals.

Respecting me by calling me MAM {my heart feels}!

You've blessed me and others you'll see.

Thank you for giving me this opportunity.

May your life be full of laughter and love.

The main person to thank is the Lord above!!!

Your friend

Claudine Donaldson

www.ingramcontent.com/pod-product-compliance
Lightning Source LLC
Chambersburg PA
CBHW040746110726
47973CB00012B/194